BALTIMORE MEMORIES II

THE EARLY YEARS, 1940s AND 1950s

THE BALTIMORE SUN MEDIA GROUP

Acknowledgments

The following organizations have contributed greatly to this project:

Photos curated by Brooke Horn

Published by Pediment Publishing, a division of The Pediment Group, Inc.
www.pediment.com. Printed in the United States of America.

LEFT: Trolleys and traffic on Fayette Street, circa 1930.
COLLECTION 117, UNIVERSITY OF MARYLAND, BALTIMORE COUNTY

Foreword

The Baltimore Sun is proud to present its second installment of *Baltimore Memories*, a collection of photographs highlighting the early years, the 1940s and the 1950s.

Like our first publication in 2017 of historic images from *Baltimore Sun* archives, the following pages showcase some of the best photographs from this organization's finest journalists. In addition to our own work throughout the years, this collection includes contributions from the Maryland Historical Society and the Enoch Pratt Free Library, the University of Maryland, Baltimore County, and the Baltimore County Public Library. And we have included many images provided by families around the region who shared their own cherished memories of Baltimore and the surrounding areas.

As a Baltimore native, I looked at the faces and places from yesteryear and admired the courage of Baltimoreans who helped fight for civil rights, felt the pain of the many people who suffered through natural disasters, and shared the celebrations of those who helped to achieve milestones in education around Maryland. Among some of the history you will find on these pages are a visit from President Franklin D. Roosevelt in 1936; Babe Ruth watching a polo match in 1936; a Goucher College field hockey game from 1943; an Enoch Pratt Free Library book wagon visiting a Baltimore street in 1945; Light Street flooding as a result of Hurricane Connie in 1955; and policewomen practicing gun skills in 1956.

Since 1837 when the first edition of *The Sun* was published, our journalists have been informing readers by chronicling the news, the people, and the personalities that help make this city so unique. Ever since those first copies were printed and sold for a penny each, *The Sun*'s mission has remained in part to help tell the Baltimore story. In 1901 as technology evolved, *The Baltimore Sun* printed its first photograph and our pages have included images each day of the people and places of Baltimore and the region.

Looking back on this history helps to better explain who we are, how we got here, and where we are going as a community. I hope you will enjoy these images as much as I did. They showcase the scenes of Baltimore and all the joys, sorrows, achievements, and challenges that we have experienced here. So much has changed during the years but in many ways some things remain the same. These images help you see a little more of old Baltimore and Maryland and how that history shaped our modern city and state.

Trif Alatzas
Publisher & Editor-in-Chief
Baltimore Sun Media Group

Table of Contents

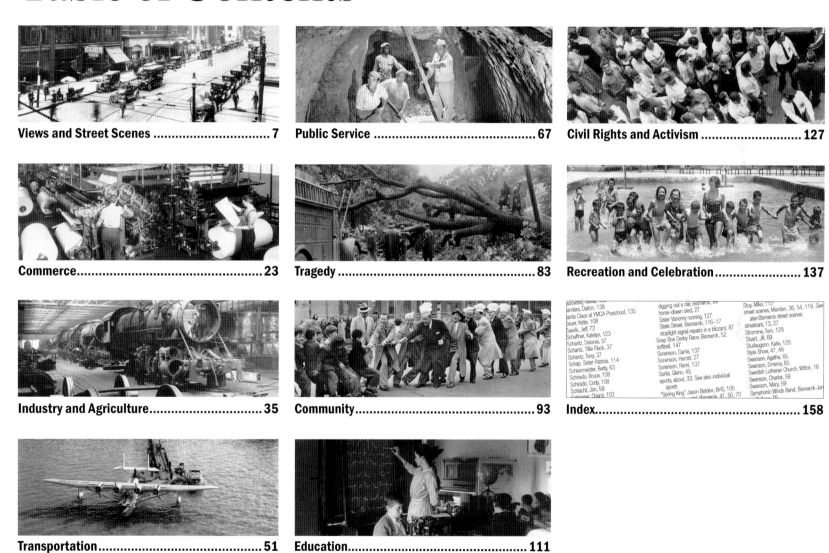

OPPOSITE: Battle Monument in front of Baltimore City Courthouse on North Calvert Street, early 1900s. The monument was completed in 1825. It was listed on the National Register of Historic Places on June 4, 1973. BALTIMORE SUN MEDIA GROUP

CHAPTER ONE

Views and Street Scenes

Thanks to the 1904 fire, downtown Baltimore was filled with newly constructed buildings by 1910. Soon the city's skyline would have three major landmarks: the Tower Building on Baltimore Street, the Emerson Drug Company's headquarters with its Bromo Seltzer bottle, and the Baltimore Trust Company's 1929 art deco landmark at 10 Light Street.

The city welcomed another downtown presence, the McCormick spice plant. It faced the harbor and offered visitors an English tea room experience.

The harbor remained a busy and hard-working port. Bay steamboats called at the Pratt and Light Street piers. The city was growing and while European immigration slowed in the 1920s, migration from the South increased to Baltimore.

The time between the wars saw the emergence of a strong and enlarged downtown shopping district. The city's department stores enlarged their sales floors and added extra floors. The corner of Howard and Lexington streets became a shoppers' destination — not only for clothes and household goods, but for entertainment as well.

The retail stores were intermixed with major movie theaters so that a trip downtown could include a matinée as well.

Dozens of other small shops, including all the national five-and-dime variety stores, established downtown outlets. Added into this mix were shoe repair businesses, hatters, lunchrooms, and restaurants. New hotels arrived too — the Lord Baltimore, the Emerson, and the Southern, which joined Charles Street's Hotel Belvedere as destinations for travelers and dining patrons in search of a good meal.

The streets were filled with pedestrians who passed by the newest addition to the street scene — the neon signs that brought rainbow colors to city streets at night.

In the 1920s the city had three newspapers — *The Sun*, *The Baltimore News*, and *The Baltimore Post*. A nickel bought you all three.

It was also a time when the city's population still traveled by streetcar and bus, although the suburbs were well established and growing. Railroad travel remained brisk and passengers boarded trains at Pennsylvania, Mount Royal, and Camden stations, as well as smaller rail stops. Air travel was in its infancy and would not become fully established until the years following World War II. Baltimore was at this time an old city beginning to adapt to new ways.

—*Jacques Kelly*

OPPOSITE: North Eutaw Street, 1921. The Hippodrome Theatre (center) was showing *The Kid* starring Charles Chaplin, Edna Purviance, and Jackie Coogan. Built in 1914, it was designed by Thomas W. Lamb. BALTIMORE SUN MEDIA GROUP

ABOVE: Baltimore Street east of Liberty Street decorated for troops returning from World War I, May 28, 1919. BALTIMORE SUN MEDIA GROUP

TOP: Baltimore viewed from Federal Hill, 1865. BALTIMORE SUN MEDIA GROUP

OPPOSITE: Inner Harbor looking north on Light Street, October 28, 1920. BALTIMORE SUN MEDIA GROUP

RIGHT: Hanover Street Bridge (renamed Vietnam Veterans Memorial Bridge in 1993) spanning the middle branch of the Patapsco River, August 6, 1923. Designed by J. E. Greiner Company and completed in 1916, it replaced a mile-long bridge built in 1856. BALTIMORE SUN MEDIA GROUP

OPPOSITE: Baltimore inner harbor, July 2, 1926. COLLECTION 117, UNIVERSITY OF MARYLAND, BALTIMORE COUNTY

BELOW RIGHT: Looking north on Cathedral Street from Franklin Street, 1923. BALTIMORE SUN MEDIA GROUP

ABOVE: Traffic on Pratt Street, circa 1930. BALTIMORE SUN MEDIA GROUP

ABOVE LEFT: Looking south from the top floor of Belvedere Hotel, March 24, 1930. BALTIMORE SUN MEDIA GROUP

OPPOSITE: The Washington Monument at Mount Vernon Place, circa 1930. The Peabody Institute is on the right. BALTIMORE SUN MEDIA GROUP

LEFT: View from Belvedere Avenue looking toward Mt. Washington, November 17, 1931. COLLECTION 117, UNIVERSITY OF MARYLAND, BALTIMORE COUNTY

ABOVE: Holiday shoppers on Howard Street, December 13, 1933. BALTIMORE SUN MEDIA GROUP

RIGHT: Fayette Street, September 27, 1936. Phoenix Shot Tower is in the background. Construction on the tower finished in 1828. Originally owned by the Merchants' Shot Tower Company, they ceased production in 1892.
COLLECTION 117, UNIVERSITY OF MARYLAND, BALTIMORE COUNTY

OPPOSITE LEFT: Patterson Park Pagoda, spring 1939. Originally known as the Patterson Park Observatory, it was designed by Charles H. Latrobe and built on Hampstead Hill in 1891. BALTIMORE SUN MEDIA GROUP

OPPOSITE TOP RIGHT: The north end of Hanover street looking south from a building on the southwest corner of Hanover and Fayette Streets, August 1, 1937.
BALTIMORE SUN MEDIA GROUP

OPPOSITE BOTTOM RIGHT: Baltimore's inner harbor, December 3, 1938.
BALTIMORE SUN MEDIA GROUP

ABOVE: Traffic and pedestrians crowding the North Howard Street intersection in Baltimore, January 15, 1941.
BALTIMORE SUN MEDIA GROUP

ABOVE RIGHT: Trolleys heading down North Howard Street in Baltimore, January 15, 1941. BALTIMORE SUN MEDIA GROUP

OPPOSITE: Holiday crowds converging at the intersection of Lexington and Howard Streets, December 15, 1947.
BALTIMORE SUN MEDIA GROUP

RIGHT: 2200 block of East Fayette Street, March 25, 1941.
COLLECTION 117, UNIVERSITY OF MARYLAND, BALTIMORE COUNTY

RIGHT: Light Street, September 18, 1944. COLLECTION 117, UNIVERSITY OF MARYLAND, BALTIMORE COUNTY

OPPOSITE: Baltimore Street looking west from Gay Street during a brownout, February 1, 1945. COLLECTION 117, UNIVERSITY OF MARYLAND, BALTIMORE COUNTY

BELOW RIGHT: Army convoy crossing Charles Street on Franklin Street, September 12, 1950. COLLECTION 117, UNIVERSITY OF MARYLAND, BALTIMORE COUNTY

BELOW: Franklin Street looking east, March 16, 1950. COLLECTION 117, UNIVERSITY OF MARYLAND, BALTIMORE COUNTY

EDISON
HOTEL
ROOMS
EMBASS
EMBASSY
Roy Logan
SHOES FOR MEN
AMERICA'S GREATEST VALUES
FROM FACTORY DIRECT TO WEARER
MILLER'S
PLAYHOUSE
DRUGS
PATENT

RIGHT: Fayette Street, December 7, 1954.
COLLECTION 117, UNIVERSITY OF MARYLAND, BALTIMORE COUNTY

OPPOSITE: Baltimore viewed from the First Presbyterian Church steeple, August 24, 1956. COLLECTION 117, UNIVERSITY OF MARYLAND, BALTIMORE COUNTY

CHAPTER TWO

Commerce

Remember those stone-age, pre-Internet days when, if you wanted something, you actually had to walk, or get in your car and drive somewhere? Oh, how quaint.

For generations of Batimoreans who came of age in the early-to-mid 20th century, the names of certain businesses will always ring a familiar bell. Reams have been written about the four department stores at the corner of Howard and Lexington streets — Hecht's, Hochschild-Kohn's, Hutzler's, and Stewart's — and how that one intersection served the shopping needs of nearly everyone (especially once they became integrated in the 1960s).

Plenty more, however, could be written about myriad other businesses that dotted the city landscape: Epstein's (which finally gave up the ghost in 1991, with the closing of its Highlandtown store), Hess Shoes (remember the sliding board in the Belvedere Avenue store?), Brager-Gutman's, Hamburger's, Kresge's, Korvette's (many a record collection owed its existence to the store's all-label sales), Read's, McCrory's, G.C. Murphy. Each had branches throughout

the city and extending out to the suburbs. Sadly, they're all gone now.

A happy sampling of where Baltimore used to shop, for everything from shoes to hats, apples to porterhouse steaks, are recalled in the following pages. Sure, times have changed. You don't find many seed and grain stores within the city limits these days. Was there really a butcher at the Hanover Market named Bucher? (Apparently so.) And every time you get one of those automated phone answering machines, where you have to sort through about a dozen possibilities before finally talking to a live person, don't you long for those banks of phone operators, ready to answer any question or find someone who could?

Which is not to imply that our city retains no links to its commercial past. People still get their food at Lexington Market, just as their ancestors were doing 200 years ago (and you can still get a mean crab cake at Faidley's, a market mainstay since 1886). We've been buying our shoes at Van Dyke & Bacon since 1938. Tochterman's has been providing bait and tackle for area fishermen

since 1916 (and earns extra kudos for its leaping-fish neon sign, a city landmark on its own). Arabbers still lead their horses up and down city streets, selling fruits and vegetables just as they have for generations.

And even some of the long-gone businesses of yore pop up on occasion, thanks to ghost ads that have outlasted the businesses they once promoted. Until just a few years ago, drivers on Liberty Street could look up and see a fading Luskin's ad, hawking a new contraption called a cellphone. Stewart's may be long gone, but its logo remains visible, high on the rear of its Howard Street headquarters. And for a real blast from the past, check out the advertisement for Gross & Stoops Carriage Works, in giant letters on the front of a building on West Saratoga Street.

So next time you're about to click "send" on that Internet order, give a thought to the old days, when buying stuff usually involved actually talking to people. You know, the old ways really weren't so bad.

—*Chris Kaltenbach*

OPPOSITE: George C. Romoser cutting meat at his stall at Cross Street Market, November 1952. BALTIMORE SUN MEDIA GROUP

ABOVE: Saloon at Edmondson and Ingleside Avenue in Catonsville, circa 1895. Included are Mr. and Mrs. Wise (Mrs. Wise later became Mrs. Werner Hanitsch). Franz "Frank" Ruff and Virginia Ruff lived there and ran the tavern.
BALTIMORE COUNTY PUBLIC LIBRARY, CATONSVILLE BRANCH

ABOVE RIGHT: John Kroner driving the Owens Feed and Grain Store delivery wagon, circa 1893. Kroner, a resident of Ingleside Avenue, drove for several Catonsville stores. Owens Feed and Grain Store was located on Frederick Road.
BALTIMORE COUNTY PUBLIC LIBRARY, CATONSVILLE BRANCH

OPPOSITE: Baltimore's iconic Lexington Market, circa 1903. Formerly known as Western Precincts Market, the famous market opened in 1782 and is one of the longest-running markets in their original location in the nation.
LIBRARY OF CONGRESS, DETROIT PUBLISHING COMPANY, LC-D401-16538

RIGHT: H. Miller's store, circa 1900. BALTIMORE SUN MEDIA GROUP

ABOVE: Heidelback grocery delivery wagon entering Ingleside Avenue next to Odd Fellows Hall, 1920s. The Heidelbach store was located at 720 Frederick Road in Catonsville. BALTIMORE COUNTY PUBLIC LIBRARY, CATONSVILLE BRANCH

RIGHT: Filling station with patriotic decorations at St. Paul and Lexington Streets, circa 1911. ENOCH PRATT FREE LIBRARY/MARYLAND'S STATE LIBRARY RESOURCE CENTER

ABOVE RIGHT: Man repairing shoes, October 10, 1933. BALTIMORE SUN MEDIA GROUP

ABOVE LEFT: Frances Leonard, Eleanor Goldsborough, and Mary Clare Chapman at the Flower Mart, May 20, 1928. BALTIMORE SUN MEDIA GROUP

LEFT: Max Richmond Store at 239 East Franklin Street, March 1926. COLLECTION 137, P75-54-N747G, UNIVERSITY OF MARYLAND, BALTIMORE COUNTY

ABOVE: Tax department in the Municipal Building, January 8, 1935. COLLECTION 117, UNIVERSITY OF MARYLAND, BALTIMORE COUNTY

RIGHT: Roadside market on North Point Road and Fayette Street, September 27, 1936. COLLECTION 117, UNIVERSITY OF MARYLAND, BALTIMORE COUNTY

ABOVE: Howard Street pedestrian traffic and Christmas shoppers, December 6, 1942. BALTIMORE SUN MEDIA GROUP

LEFT: Joseph W. Clautice and Stark making the Association of Commerce motion picture of Baltimore, March 1, 1940. BALTIMORE SUN MEDIA GROUP

RIGHT: Mending and building chairs from salvaged furniture for Goodwill Industries, February 19, 1944. BALTIMORE SUN MEDIA GROUP

OPPOSITE LEFT: Chesapeake and Potomac telephone operators at switchboards in St. Paul's building, May 29, 1950. BALTIMORE SUN MEDIA GROUP

OPPOSITE TOP RIGHT: "Abe" Rostov of Dickeyville General Store chatting with Mrs. Russ Bradley and Mrs. Charles D. Warfield, March 22, 1951. COLLECTION 117, UNIVERSITY OF MARYLAND, BALTIMORE COUNTY

OPPOSITE BOTTOM RIGHT: People waiting in line for sirloin and porterhouse steaks at the Hanover Market stall for K. J. Bucher, October 26, 1947. BALTIMORE SUN MEDIA GROUP

ABOVE: Hollins Market, October 27, 1957. The stalls were set up on Thursday, Friday, and Saturday in both summer and winter, fair weather and foul. BALTIMORE SUN MEDIA GROUP

RIGHT: Arcade Pharmacy at the corner of Hamilton Avenue and Harford Road, 1957. The pharmacy closed in 1997. BALTIMORE SUN MEDIA GROUP

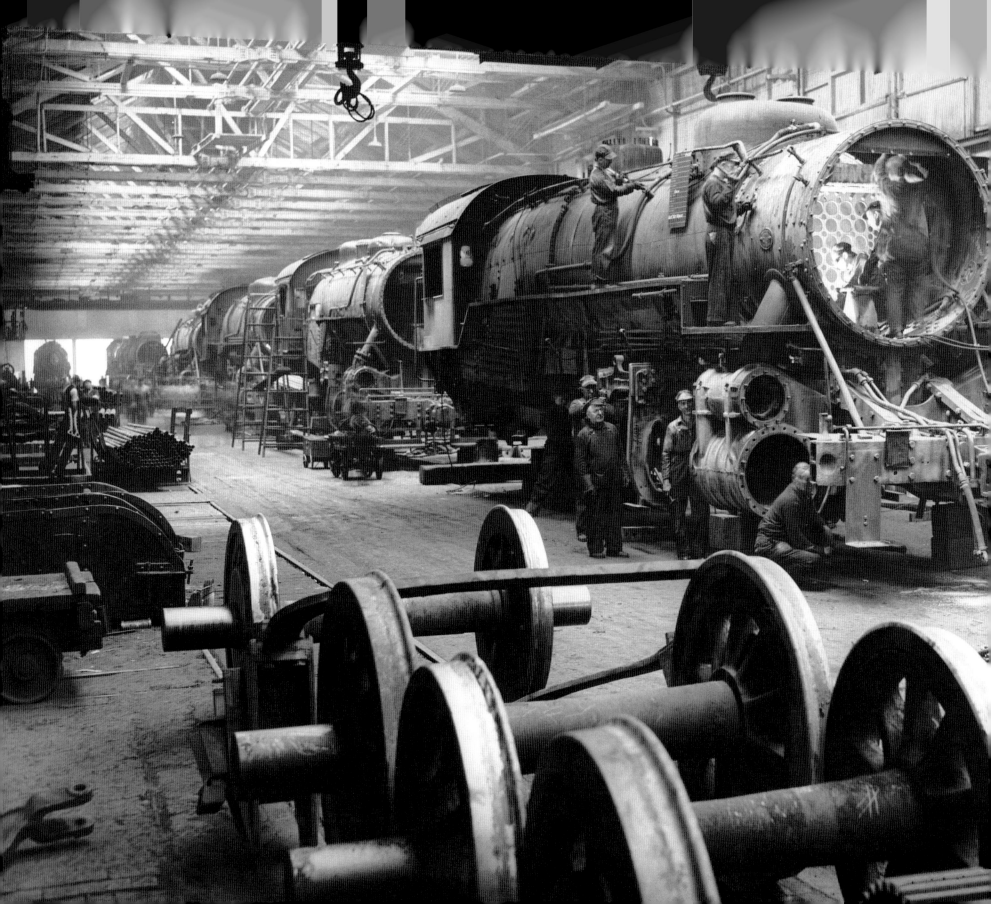

CHAPTER THREE

Industry and Agriculture

Baltimore was a working, smoky city. The call to labor began early in the morning as steam boiler whistles called men and women to jobs. Many walked or took a fairly short streetcar or bus ride to the plant gate.

Soon the mills, machine shops, and forges were humming. Steel, railroads, and the waterfront dominated the job market. Baltimore was once marked by sprawling industrial campuses — the Baltimore & Ohio Railroad shops at Mount Clare and Bethlehem Steel and its Maryland Shipbuilding and Drydock at Sparrows Point were the major employers in the years between the great world wars.

The city's superlative harbor and port facilities stimulated industrial growth. Baltimore became a city that made things — it also shopped and received them. Dotting the harbor's edge were the canneries that took the Eastern Shore of Maryland's farm produce and wrapped it in tin. The city had tin can makers too.

A whole garment-making district sprang up in the southwest section of the downtown. Immigrants who were skilled at a sewing machine turned out men's suits, overcoats, hats, and umbrellas.

The spices of the world flowed through the McCormick Light Street plant. The cinnamon scented the harbor.

The city once had a small railway that operated along city streets around the wharves. Locomotives hauled freight cars, mainly at night to avoid interference with busy daytime traffic, to deliver and retrieve the raw materials to downtown plants and industries. Other rail lines were threaded through the city — and under the city streets. Freight and passenger rail tunnels passed under major thoroughfares — Howard Street, as well as Hoffman and Winchester streets.

The push for industrialization along the harbor saw industries expand throughout Fairfield and Curtis Bay. Bulk materials, chemicals, and fertilizers could be produced and shipped out using the Patapsco River and Chesapeake Bay. An old amusement park became the Western Electric Point Breeze Works and produced cable for the Bell Telephone system. Baltimore also gave the country the crown cork — a type of bottle sealer used by the beverage industry.

The city made bricks, fancy silverware, power drills, brewed beer, and distilled rye whiskey. The newest industrial was the Glenn L. Martin Co. aircraft complex at Middle River. And Bromo Seltzer was still made, in blue bottles, in the Emerson Drug Tower.

—*Jacques Kelly*

OPPOSITE: Baltimore and Ohio's Mount Clare shop workers going over the locomotives that are in for overhaul, July 19, 1942. Without them, goods could not be delivered. BALTIMORE SUN MEDIA GROUP

ABOVE: Annie Bissie, a child laborer in the Baltimore area, 1909. Photograph by Lewis Hine. LIBRARY OF CONGRESS, LC-DIG-NCLC-00010

RIGHT: McCormick & Company, December 10, 1933. The spice and flavoring company was founded in Baltimore in 1889 and went on to become a Fortune 1000 company. BALTIMORE SUN MEDIA GROUP

ABOVE: Contour plowing on a York Road farm in Baltimore County, April 2, 1936. BALTIMORE SUN MEDIA GROUP

LEFT: Anne Arundel cantaloupes at Long Dock in Baltimore's Inner Harbor, August 2, 1937. BALTIMORE SUN MEDIA GROUP

RIGHT: Two Gulf Oil Corporation tankers, 11,000 tons each, under construction at Bethlehem Sparrows Point Shipyard, 1937. These tankers were the largest boats built in Baltimore at the time. BALTIMORE SUN MEDIA GROUP

OPPOSITE: Baltimore Brick Co., November 1938.
ENOCH PRATT FREE LIBRARY/MARYLAND'S STATE LIBRARY RESOURCE CENTER

BELOW RIGHT: Baltimore Gas and Electric Co. employee, 1936.
ENOCH PRATT FREE LIBRARY/MARYLAND'S STATE LIBRARY RESOURCE CENTER

BELOW: Worker making sausage at a meat packing plant, March 19, 1938. BALTIMORE SUN MEDIA GROUP

ABOVE: Port Covington piers in front of Gould Street plant, 1940. BALTIMORE SUN MEDIA GROUP

ABOVE RIGHT: Workers at Bethlehem Steel at Sparrows Point, April 18, 1940. BALTIMORE SUN MEDIA GROUP

OPPOSITE: Ship workers standing in front of the Liberty Ship *Samuel Chase* with a "Ships for Victory" sign in the shape of a "V," May 12, 1942. BALTIMORE SUN MEDIA GROUP

RIGHT: Workers attaching zinc plates to A. H. Bull and Company's *Cornelia* of the Bull Line in dry-dock at Key Highway, August 25, 1939. These plates protected the rudder framework from electrolysis caused by the propeller revolving. BALTIMORE SUN MEDIA GROUP

Bethlehem Fairfield Shipbuilding Company, September 9, 1942. BALTIMORE SUN MEDIA GROUP

ABOVE: Bethlehem Steel shipyard drafters, September 18, 1943. BALTIMORE SUN MEDIA GROUP

ABOVE LEFT: Working with wire at Bethlehem Steel, October 14, 1942. BALTIMORE SUN MEDIA GROUP

LEFT: Workmen shoveling wood in to heat up the blast furnaces, February 1946. BALTIMORE SUN MEDIA GROUP

RIGHT: Westinghouse Manufacturing and Repair Plant at Foster and Haven Avenues, June 30, 1949. BALTIMORE SUN MEDIA GROUP

Miss Eleanor Brady and Miss Margaretta Dorsey repairing their tractor, April 24, 1949. BALTIMORE SUN MEDIA GROUP

RIGHT: Member of the Mohawk tribe making lacrosse sticks, April 15, 1951. A single Mohawk tribe made, and a Baltimore concern sold, most of the world's supply. Smoothed by tribal elders, the younger men bore the holes for the laces. A Baltimore sporting goods firm is the sole distributor of the sticks. BALTIMORE SUN MEDIA GROUP

ABOVE: Baltimore clothing plant, May 2, 1954. Baltimore's first clothing plant was set up in 1838. In 1909, the city was the top maker of men's suits. BALTIMORE SUN MEDIA GROUP

ABOVE LEFT: Daffodil farm, April 1, 1953. BALTIMORE SUN MEDIA GROUP

LEFT: Development of egg sorting machinery at Beltsville Agriculture Research Station, April 29, 1956. BALTIMORE SUN MEDIA GROUP

RIGHT: Galvanized strip steel and the machinery to produce it in the background at Bethlehem Steel, December 26, 1956. BALTIMORE SUN MEDIA GROUP

LEFT: Members of the Japanese Industrial Water Supply and Utilization Specialists Study touring Baltimore Harbor on the USS *Baltimore*, July 28, 1959. Peter Polimeni, foreign commerce representative, MD Port Authority is on right pointing. BALTIMORE SUN MEDIA GROUP

BELOW: Bethlehem Steel Company, January 18, 1957.
BALTIMORE SUN MEDIA GROUP

CHAPTER FOUR

Transportation

Traveling in Maryland remained pretty much as it had before World War II with major options being road, rail, and Chesapeake Bay steamboat. Aviation was still in its infancy.

The major north-south highway through the state was U.S. Route 1, often referred to as "America's Main Street," with the major east-west route being U.S. 40, also known as "The National Road," that was authorized by Congress and began building westward from Cumberland in 1811.

The Baltimore & Ohio Railroad was the nation's first common carrier railroad; it was chartered in 1827 to connect Baltimore with the Ohio River at Wheeling, W.Va. The B & O's trackage eventually stretched to Chicago, St. Louis, Philadelphia, and New York. Baltimore passengers boarded the steamcars at Camden Station and later Mount Royal station.

The Pennsylvania Railroad was the B & O's flanged-wheel-on-fixed-rail competitor between Washington and New York. Its passengers boarded at Baltimore's Penn Station and had more options in a greater field of passenger trains that afforded a downtown arrival on Manhattan Island.

While certainly venerated, the B & O's much smaller field of trains, which ended their run in Jersey City, meant that passengers had to transfer to the Central Railroad of New Jersey ferry for a swift passage across the Hudson River to Lower Manhattan.

But times were changing.

Travel patterns had been disrupted by the war when unnecessary civilian train travel was discouraged because of the need to move those serving in the armed forces between bases and ports of embarkation. Trains were often jammed with travelers and standing up between points became a normal wartime experience.

Because of the necessity of steel and rubber for the war effort, no new automobiles were built, as automakers converted their plants to build tanks, trucks, and airplanes.

When the war ended in 1945, pent-up energy brought on by gas rationing, re-treaded tires, and memories of overpacked public conveyances of every description during the war years, the lure and call of the open road beckoned.

Dinah Shore, in a Chevrolet commercial seemed to say it all: "See the USA in a Chevrolet, America is asking you to call."

Over the next two decades, the American travel landscape would be altered by the launching in the mid-1950s of the Interstate highway system. Locally, I-695, also known

as the Baltimore Beltway, would eventually ring the city.

The Harbor Tunnel which sped traffic under the city rather than through it, opened in 1957. Nearly, 30 years later, the Fort McHenry Tunnel started collecting its first tolls. In the first six hours of its July 30, 1952, opening, some 2,300 cars motored across the Chesapeake Bay Bridge, connecting the Western and Eastern Shores.

When it opened in 1961, the 17.9 mile Jones Falls Expressway linking the city with Baltimore County began a tradition of traffic jams that continues to this day. More roads in the coming years would include Interstates 95, 895, and 395.

As travel by plane became more reliable and a quicker way to go, old Harbor Field in Dundalk, which had hosted the majestic Boeing Clippers and other commercial aircraft, became a thing of the past when Friendship Airport — today Baltimore-Washington International Thurgood Marshall Airport — opened in 1950.

There were transportation casualties caused mostly by the roads and turnpikes that paralleled them that resulted in the termination of service.

On April 26, 1958, ironically aptly named B & O engineer Michael F. Goodnight

OPPOSITE: Baltimore Municipal Airport, Maryland National Guard air unit, Pan-American clipper, November 17, 1937.
ENOCH PRATT FREE LIBRARY/MARYLAND'S STATE LIBRARY RESOURCE CENTER

RIGHT: Participants in the first Baltimore Auto Race, circa 1900. ENOCH PRATT FREE LIBRARY/ MARYLAND'S STATE LIBRARY RESOURCE CENTER

OPPOSITE: First trolley overhead line car of United Railways auto division on North Avenue, 1910. COLLECTION 117, UNIVERSITY OF MARYLAND, BALTIMORE COUNTY

eased the last northbound Royal Blue — Baltimore's beloved daylight passenger train — up to the bumper post in the Central Railroad's Communipaw Terminal in Jersey City. A day later, the B & O ended all passenger service north of Washington.

In 1958, the old Ma & Pa, more formally known as the Maryland & Pennsylvania Railroad, ended service between Baltimore and York, Pa., while the Western Maryland

Railway exited the passenger business the next year.

The Old Bay Line steamers City of Richmond and City of Norfolk that had connected Baltimore and Hampton Roads, Va., tied up for the last time on April 14, 1962. The Baltimore Steam Packet Co., which had been in business since 1840, was no more.

The auto wasn't through exacting its revenge. The Baltimore Transit Co. and

its predecessor companies that had been operating streetcars for more than a century brought the Baltimore trolley era to a close on November 3, 1963, when it operated its last car and took 425 miles of trackage out of service.

Streetcars, on a much limited basis, would not return until 1991 with the birth of the Hunt Valley-Glen Burnie Light Rail line.

—Frederick N. Rasmussen

ABOVE: American aviators Amelia Earhart and Glenn L. Martin, November 13, 1930. BALTIMORE SUN MEDIA GROUP

ABOVE RIGHT: Painting traffic lines on Twenty-Fifth Street from Greenmount Avenue to Harford Road, May 1, 1924. BALTIMORE SUN MEDIA GROUP

RIGHT: Children standing in awe of a locomotive at the Fair of the Iron Horse, the Baltimore & Ohio Railroad centenary exhibition and pageant of the railroad, October 1927. BALTIMORE SUN MEDIA GROUP

Maryland National Guard plane No. 7 flying over Baltimore, 1931. ENOCH PRATT FREE LIBRARY/MARYLAND'S STATE LIBRARY RESOURCE CENTER

ABOVE: The *Atlantic*, a Baltimore & Ohio Railroad locomotive, 1933. BALTIMORE SUN MEDIA GROUP

ABOVE RIGHT: Baltimore & Ohio Railroad engine, May 19, 1936. BALTIMORE SUN MEDIA GROUP

OPPOSITE: Mrs. William H. Shehan smashing a champagne bottle to christen a Trans World Airlines plane, November 30, 1936. Also present are Mayor Howard W. Jackson and Mrs. Jackson.
BALTIMORE SUN MEDIA GROUP

RIGHT: The United Fruit Company's Great White Fleet steamer *I. K. Ward* docked in Baltimore Harbor, November 11, 1933. BALTIMORE SUN MEDIA GROUP

ABOVE: Parking lot at Guliford Avenue and Saratoga Street, January 18, 1938. Notice the elevated trestle in the background. BALTIMORE SUN MEDIA GROUP

ABOVE LEFT: The USS *Tolchester* waiting her turn at the Maryland Drydock in Fairfield, May 22, 1938. BALTIMORE SUN MEDIA GROUP

OPPOSITE: Baltimore Municipal Airport on opening day, November 17, 1941. Construction originally began for development of a seaplane base in 1929, and the airport closed in 1960. ENOCH PRATT FREE LIBRARY/MARYLAND'S STATE LIBRARY RESOURCE CENTER

LEFT: Logan Field in Dundalk, 1939. BALTIMORE SUN MEDIA GROUP

ABOVE: Passengers exiting streetcars, November 27, 1944. <small>BALTIMORE SUN MEDIA GROUP</small>

ABOVE RIGHT: Streetcar conductors, January 1943. Included are Mrs. A. A. Rawls, Mrs. C. Wilkens, Mrs. H. P. Rohrbaugh, Mrs. R. Melchior, and Mrs. G. H. Russel. <small>BALTIMORE SUN MEDIA GROUP</small>

RIGHT: B & O Railroad train of tank cars crossing the Thomas Viaduct between Relay and Elk Ridge, 1942. <small>GLYNDON L. BAILEY</small>

Christine Smith of Allegany County enjoying a meal in a railroad diner car with companions, December 29, 1946. BALTIMORE SUN MEDIA GROUP

ABOVE: Couple traveling on a Baltimore & Ohio train with their dog, July 14, 1950. COLLECTION 117, UNIVERSITY OF MARYLAND, BALTIMORE COUNTY

ABOVE RIGHT: Curtis Bay Company tugboats loading up for tug men conference outside the United Fruit Company, February 15, 1946. BALTIMORE SUN MEDIA GROUP

RIGHT: People waiting to get on the bus at Liberty and Lexington Streets, May 27, 1947. BALTIMORE SUN MEDIA GROUP

LEFT: Construction and repair crews working on the 600 block of Clement Street, July 9, 1951. COLLECTION 117, UNIVERSITY OF MARYLAND, BALTIMORE COUNTY

BELOW LEFT: Working on the Clement Street cavern, July 18, 1951. COLLECTION 117, UNIVERSITY OF MARYLAND, BALTIMORE COUNTY

BELOW: Newly completed platforms at Camden Station, September 24, 1951. COLLECTION 117, UNIVERSITY OF MARYLAND, BALTIMORE COUNTY

RIGHT: Traffic on Potee Street, January 28, 1953. COLLECTION 117, UNIVERSITY OF MARYLAND, BALTIMORE COUNTY

OPPOSITE: Well-wishers bidding fond adieu to the old No. 9 trolley line as the last streetcar starts from Catonsville Junction to Ellicott City, June 20, 1955. BALTIMORE SUN MEDIA GROUP

BELOW RIGHT: Robert Powerlane at the Shipping Board of Seaman's home, November 12, 1954. BALTIMORE SUN MEDIA GROUP

CHAPTER FIVE

Public Service

By all accounts, it was a normal day on the 600 block of East Clement Street in Federal Hill on June 10, 1951, when at around 2 p.m. a tiny crack appeared on the front of a house at 612. But not long after, that sliver turned into an ugly scar ripping through mortar like a fault line and then more and more, and the house slipped into the subterranean pit below — soon to be joined by its neighbors at 608 to 614. Police arrived to block off the street. Families were evacuated. One by one, officers cleared the block, helping people scramble to safety.

The cave-in that swallowed five houses was ultimately blamed on an old tunnel from the previous century that had been used to collect clay to make fire bricks but then forgotten. It took hundreds of tons of gravel and sand from nearby Brooklyn to fill it. But no lives were lost and it was but one example of how Baltimore was evolving in the years after World War II, becoming more sophisticated, more professional, more urban, more educated. Its police and fire services reflected that change.

For the Baltimore City Fire Department, the red letter day was the evening of February 16, 1955, when the Tru-Fit Clothing Company on West Baltimore Street downtown burst into flames, quickly growing into a nine-alarm blaze that took the lives of a half-dozen firefighters. The loss devastated the city but it took several days before people realized just how much families had sacrificed — aside from modest $1,500 life insurance policies and $500 funeral payments, the families of the fallen had little to maintain their households — until a fund was launched by *The Baltimore Sun* and other civic leaders, raising $169,000 to supplement pensions and savings. The cause of the fire was never determined, although the case is technically considered still open.

Not long after that, Baltimore started getting serious about providing for the dependents of firefighters and police who are killed in the line of duty. Such reforms followed other changes in the public service sector as city residents began expecting more training and professionalism from those in civil service. After the attack on Pearl Harbor, for example, then-Police Commissioner Robert F. Stanton established a police "auxiliary" to assist the force as trained volunteers.

In 1943, African-American officers were finally allowed to wear uniforms; Patrolman James H. Butler Jr. was the first African-American made sergeant in 1947 (the first woman to make sergeant came ten years earlier). The city's original crime lab opened one year later and the first K9 unit was created in 1956. Readers of *The Sun* marveled over the first cadets to graduate from the city's new police academy in 1950 — in their 90 days or 396 hours of instruction, they'd learned about psychology, criminal investigation, and obstetrics.

These were, after all, the years when public service was seen as a noble calling and the men and women returning from duty in the Pacific or Europe were comfortable donning a uniform to enforce parking meters (the first of which arrived in 1955 on Charles Street), or deliver mail or patrol a beat. For many African-Americans, government service provided job opportunities not yet open to them in the private sector of a still highly segregated city.

—Peter Jensen

OPPOSITE: Workers digging in the main cavern below Clement Street, July 6, 1951. Highway Department foreman Michael Jorio is on the right.
COLLECTION 117, UNIVERSITY OF MARYLAND, BALTIMORE COUNTY

MAIN ENTRANCE
Delegates - Alternat[es]
WORKING PRESS
SECTIONS 2-3-4-5-6-7-8-9-27-28-29
44-45-61-62-63-6[4]

ABOVE: Catonsville Fire Department, circa 1915. Included are Gideon Smith, "Hats" Marsberger, Al Watterman, and Gus Peters.
COLLECTION OF BALTIMORE COUNTY PUBLIC LIBRARY, CATONSVILLE BRANCH

ABOVE LEFT: Spring Grove State Hospital occupational therapy in the Needlepoint Room, circa 1914. BALTIMORE COUNTY PUBLIC LIBRARY, CATONSVILLE BRANCH

OPPOSITE: Democratic National Convention in the Fifth Regiment Armory, 1912. LIBRARY OF CONGRESS, LC-H261- 1520

LEFT: Spring Grove State Hospital, circa 1900.
COLLECTION OF BALTIMORE COUNTY PUBLIC LIBRARY, CATONSVILLE BRANCH

ABOVE: U.S. Army Ordnance Depot at Curtis Bay, 1920s. BALTIMORE SUN MEDIA GROUP

RIGHT: Servicemen using a typewriter at the Red Cross Institute for the Blind, circa 1918. The Red Cross Institute for the Blind was established in 1917 to help soldiers blinded in WWI adjust to civilian life back home. In 1922, the facility was transferred to the U.S. Veterans Bureau and then became known as Evergreen Vocational Training School. LIBRARY OF CONGRESS, LC-DIG-ANRC-02472

ABOVE: Junior Fire Department, October 8, 1925.
BALTIMORE SUN MEDIA GROUP

ABOVE LEFT: Sgt. Karl Ducka and Sgt. Joseph L. Bonville with Marines bulldog prior to the Fire Department vs. Marines football game, November 20, 1933. BALTIMORE SUN MEDIA GROUP

LEFT: Baltimore Police Department patrol wagon used in a parade, 1933. BALTIMORE SUN MEDIA GROUP

ABOVE: Coast Guardsmen taking a rowing class, 1940. They left Curtis Bay Coast Guard Station after completing a six-week training course. BALTIMORE SUN MEDIA GROUP

ABOVE LEFT: Catonsville Fire Company in front of the Catonsville Fire Department and Police Station, 1938. BALTIMORE SUN MEDIA GROUP

OPPOSITE: President Franklin D. Roosevelt smiling as he addresses the Young Democratic Club in Baltimore, April 13, 1936. LIBRARY OF CONGRESS, LC-DIG-HEC-47220

LEFT: Parade for the Firemen Marine Corps football game, October 31, 1938.
BALTIMORE SUN MEDIA GROUP

LEFT: Maryland State Police Training School, May 26, 1946.
BALTIMORE SUN MEDIA GROUP

OPPOSITE: H. F. Schulteis instructing Maryland State Police training recruits W. C. Dykes, Ed McGee, Robert Bowersox, and Leslie B. Thompson in motorcycles, August 13, 1941.
BALTIMORE SUN MEDIA GROUP

BELOW: Mrs. Crouch's Kindercraft Kindergarten class visiting the Catonsville Fire Department No. 4 on Frederick Road at Eggers Lane, circa 1946. Included are firemen Herbert Morsberger and Ernie Elgert.
BALTIMORE COUNTY PUBLIC LIBRARY, CATONSVILLE BRANCH

ABOVE: Corporal S. N. Cow of the Maryland State Troopers demonstrating how radar works to Richard Hartman of the Auto Club of Maryland and John Keatts of Washington D.C., June 7, 1950. BALTIMORE SUN MEDIA GROUP

RIGHT: Members of Co. 147 kissing their girls goodbye as the train begins to depart Camden Station, August 30, 1950. COLLECTION 117, UNIVERSITY OF MARYLAND, BALTIMORE COUNTY

Police officers using the Electromatic Speed Meter to identify speeding motorists, June 11, 1950

RIGHT: Postman Richard Coleman delivering mail to neighbors Mrs. Henry A. Naylor Jr. and Mrs. Luther Sieck (holding Alan Naylor) in Dickeyville, February 12, 1951.
COLLECTION 117, UNIVERSITY OF MARYLAND, BALTIMORE COUNTY

ABOVE RIGHT: State Police Expert Mike Kratz comparing the cast of a shoe print made at a crime scene with a shoe that belongs to a suspect in the case, October 9, 1955. BALTIMORE SUN MEDIA GROUP

ABOVE LEFT: Baltimore's policewomen, May 4, 1953. BALTIMORE SUN MEDIA GROUP

LEFT: Mrs. Margaret McDaniel and Officer Jerome Klein on duty at Twenty-Second Street, September 30, 1952.
COLLECTION 117, UNIVERSITY OF MARYLAND, BALTIMORE COUNTY

LEFT: Baltimore County police lining up to be measured for their new police uniforms, April 30, 1958. Ellis Cohen was measuring officer Richard Taylor of the Fullerton Station.
COLLECTION 117, UNIVERSITY OF MARYLAND, BALTIMORE COUNTY

OPPOSITE: Red Cross instructor Robert Greyson showing police how to use a grappling hook to retrieve a body from the lake at Druid Hill Park, April 19, 1956. BALTIMORE SUN MEDIA GROUP

BELOW LEFT: Policewomen practicing gun skills, February 9, 1956. From left: Elsie S. Jarvis, Mary E. Holden, Sergeant Ethyle T. Diven.
BALTIMORE SUN MEDIA GROUP

CHAPTER SIX

Tragedy

Some 7,00 spectators gathered on March 6, 1952, at the Fifth Regiment Armory to take in Sonja Henie's "1952 Ice Revue."

The three-time Olympic champion, who was known as the "Pavlova on Ice," was about to go on at 8:25 p.m. when a loud crack that was described like that of a "train passing beneath the building," echoed throughout the building.

Hastily built temporary bleachers gave way and dumped those attending the show about 15 feet to the floor. Some 300 were injured — 30 seriously.

Henie, who ended the ice revue the next year, never again performed in Baltimore.

But if you had to pick a banner year for deadly fires and hurricanes in the city, the honors would go to 1955.

At 9:02 p.m. on February 16, 1955, the first of nine alarms was sounded from Box 12 at East Baltimore and Frederick streets, in the center of The Block. A second followed at 9:06 p.m., which was followed by a third at 9:13 p.m.

Firefighters raced to the Tru-Fit Clothing Co. building at 507–509 E. Baltimore St., and upon their arrival were greeted by great billowing clouds of smoke that emanated from its basement. Hundreds of firefighters finally got the stubborn fire under control by 10:45 p.m. and finally were able to enter the three-story building.

Five minutes later, the rear roof of the building and its walls collapsed with a roar, trapping firefighters under tons of debris.

The catastrophe killed six firefighters: Battalion Chief Francis O'Brien, Joseph C. Hanley, Rudolph A. Machovec, Richard E. Melzer, William W. Barnes, and Anthony Reinsfelder.

While the fire was not officially ruled an arson, Tru-Fit's owner was able to collect insurance for the loss of the building and inventory.

Sixty-three years later, the Baltimore City Fire Department file on what caused the tragic fire is still open.

Recalled as the "twin" hurricanes, Diane and Connie barreled into Maryland, making August 1955 the city's wettest month with 18.35 inches of rain.

The first hurricane to arrive was Connie on August 13, which dumped 8.49 inches of rain on the city during a 24-hour period. Winds reached more than 60 mph. and tides of more than four feet sent harbor water into city streets. The *Levin J. Marvel*, a vacation schooner sailing the Chesapeake Bay, was caught in the maw of the storm, and capsized with a loss of 14 souls.

By the time Connie blew itself out in Canada, 41 had died, and for Maryland farmers, it was the end of one of the worst droughts to hit the state in years.

Barely able to recover, the state was hit four days later by Hurricane Diane, accompanied by tropical rains that sent the Potomac River on a rampage, cresting at 22.5 feet in Cumberland. By the time Diane rolled into the Atlantic southeast of Atlantic City, 179 people had lost their lives.

The following year again brought disasters.

Sunday, January 29, 1956, would be remembered by newspaper reporters, editors, and photographers as a trifecta of major breaking news stories.

At 12:01 a.m., some 2,000 Baltimore Transit Co. motormen and bus drivers walked off the job after labor negotiations collapsed, attempting to increase the hourly wage from $1.90 to $2.00 along with a reduced work week, and brought public transit to a halt.

Then the news arrived in the at *The Sun*'s city room that H.L. Mencken, the famed newspaperman, author and editor, had died at his Hollins Street home in the early hours.

In the afternoon, a quickly moving fire swept Arundel Park Hall on Belle Grove

---

OPPOSITE: Crew working to remove a tree fallen across Garrison Boulevard, June 13, 1951. COLLECTION 117, UNIVERSITY OF MARYLAND, BALTIMORE COUNTY

Road in Brooklyn Park, where 1,200 men, women, and children had gathered to attend an oyster roast sponsored by Brooklyn's St. Rose of Lima Roman Catholic Church.

The fire was noticed at 4:55 p.m. when smoke appeared coming from a cornice between the concrete block and wooden kitchen roof, and raced through a false ceiling above those sitting at tables below.

A stampede erupted as the panicked crowd ran for the doors and windows. What they didn't know was that the hall's largest door through which 250 people could pass in a minute, had been locked to keep out non-paying freeloaders.

Fire engines from 10 companies including Baltimore, raced to the scene, and when it was over in three minutes, 10 women had lost their lives. Andrew Brady, 57, a retired firefighter who worked at the hall as a special policeman and had remained behind helping guests to escape, died a week later of severe burns at South Baltimore General Hospital.

—*Frederick N. Rasmussen*

ABOVE: Baltimore Street west of St. Paul after the Great Baltimore Fire of 1904. LIBRARY OF CONGRESS, LC-USZ62-133946

LEFT: Barge *Loveland* being towed by *Solarina* in Chesapeake Bay, January 27, 1936. BALTIMORE SUN MEDIA GROUP

OPPOSITE: Baltimore Fire Department truck and a streetcar after a violent collision, November 1, 1934. BALTIMORE SUN MEDIA GROUP

RIGHT: William G. Scarlett Company fire, July 8, 1948.
BALTIMORE SUN MEDIA GROUP

LEFT: Manufacturers Clothing Outlet fire, February 6, 1950. BALTIMORE SUN MEDIA GROUP

BELOW: Derailed cars under Greenmount Avenue, 1948. BALTIMORE SUN MEDIA GROUP

Accident between a streetcar and an automobile near the Edmondson Avenue and Hilton Street underpass, June 5, 1953. BALTIMORE SUN MEDIA GROUP

ABOVE LEFT: Head-on collision caused by an early snowstorm, November 29, 1953. BALTIMORE SUN MEDIA GROUP

LEFT: Samuel Mills securing his antique auto in front of his house at 427 South Stricker Street in preparation for a Hurricane Connie, August 1955. BALTIMORE SUN MEDIA GROUP

ABOVE: Flooding on Light Street caused by Hurricane Connie, August 14, 1955. BALTIMORE SUN MEDIA GROUP

LEFT: Carlins Park fire, November 18, 1955. COLLECTION 117, UNIVERSITY OF MARYLAND, BALTIMORE COUNTY

CHAPTER SEVEN

Community

From Fells Point in the 18th century to Port Covington in the 21st, Baltimore has always been a city defined by its neighborhoods. Sure, people are proud to say they hail from these parts and argue fiercely to protect their city's honor. But they're likely to argue far more fiercely when it comes to defending the honor of Hampden, or Cherry Hill, or Highlandtown. From Roland Park to Brooklyn, Dickeyville to Belair-Edison, communities in this city are fiercely proud of who they are, and while they may be welcoming to outsiders, it's with the understanding that you'd better not unduly mess with what was here before you.

Perhaps no period shines a spotlight on the peculiarities and profundities of Baltimore's crazy quilt of communities better than the mid-20th century. For one thing, there were plenty of photographers and photojournalists around to record them, working for *The Sun* and *The Evening Sun*, as well as for the *Baltimore News-Post, Baltimore American, Baltimore Afro-American, Baltimore Jewish Times* and plenty of other news journals.

As the population became more mobile, thanks to the prominence of the automobile and the ease of migrating to the suburbs, identity became ever more important. Sometimes, that wasn't exactly a good thing; witness the red-lining of city neighborhoods, unofficial boundaries set to keep minorities confined to certain areas. But more mobility meant people felt freer to explore, to seek out areas of the city they may never have visited. And increasingly, they came to appreciate what they found.

And what was at the center of these neighborhoods? Churches, synagogues, and other places of worship, for the most part — places where people congregated naturally, and felt safe. Sometimes an industry would have a community grow up around it — witness Sparrows Point, or Curtis Bay, or Locust Point. Often, a community would serve as an ethnic enclave — Highlandtown and its environs for the Greeks (where a neighborhood called Greektown still thrives), the Federal Hill area for the Germans (once one of Baltimore's largest immigrant communities, which explains why the German-language

Baltimore Correspondent survived into the 1970s), the Pennsylvania Avenue corridor for African-Americans, once home to a culture as vibrant as anything New York's Harlem had to offer.

Happily, many of the neighborhoods brought to such vivid life by the photographs on these pages continue to celebrate what brought their communities together in the first place, and what makes them distinctive. On these pages, you'll see glimpses of Baltimore's polyglot heritage which continues to be celebrated in everything from the Sowebo Arts and Music Festival to the Pigtown Festival, from Little Italy's St. Anthony Festival to the AFRAM Festival in Druid Hill Park to the Ukrainian Festival at St. Michael Ukrainian Catholic Church and the Russian Festival at Holy Trinity Russian Orthodox Church.

Ah, Baltimore — a city that revels in the eclectic!

—Chris Kaltenbach, the descendant of proud German immigrants who settled near Federal Hill

---

OPPOSITE: Young boys prevailing against the adults in a game of tug-of-war during a visit from the East Baltimore Boys Club, May 1952. COLLECTION 117, UNIVERSITY OF MARYLAND, BALTIMORE COUNTY

Newsboys in front of *Baltimore News* circulation substation No. 15 at 1725 Bank Street, circa 1913.

LEFT: Henry Louis Mencken holding a copy of *The American Mercury*, a magazine he and George Jean Nathan founded in 1924, among a group of supporters. The magazine featured writing by some of the most influential writers in the United States in the 1920s and 1930s. BALTIMORE SUN MEDIA GROUP

BELOW LEFT: Women's Quilting Club of Dundalk, 1930. Included are Mrs. H. W. Churchill, Mrs. Harry Fisher, Mrs. Harry Bartley, Mrs. Ernest Bechtel, Mrs. Waldo Cross, Mrs. Calder Little, and Mrs. Lewis Dennick. BALTIMORE SUN MEDIA GROUP

BELOW: Employees working in *The Sun* newspaper building at Baltimore and Charles Streets, November 20, 1929.
BALTIMORE SUN MEDIA GROUP

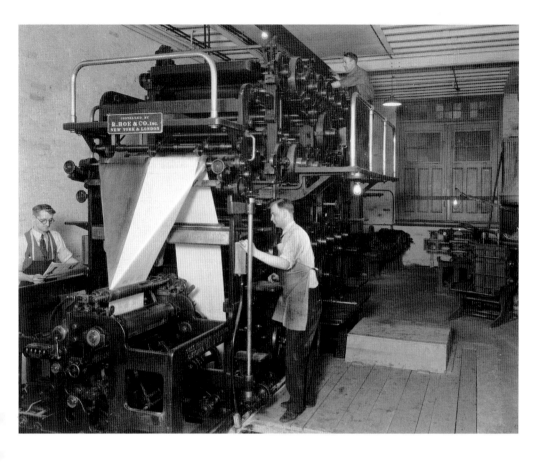

ABOVE: Mrs. Joseph Villa and Rosalee taking a walk on Eastern Avenue, June 14, 1942.
BALTIMORE SUN MEDIA GROUP

ABOVE LEFT: Baltimore *Correspondent* pressroom, circa 1937.
ENOCH PRATT FREE LIBRARY/MARYLAND'S STATE LIBRARY RESOURCE CENTER

OPPOSITE: Homes destroyed for the widening of Fayette Street near Aisquith Street,
January 10, 1937. COLLECTION 117, UNIVERSITY OF MARYLAND, BALTIMORE COUNTY

LEFT: Hampden Presbyterian Church Picnic at Wyman Park, 1943. BALTIMORE SUN MEDIA GROUP

Enoch Pratt Free Library/Maryland's State Library Resource Center book wagon visiting the 1000 block of Dallas Street in Baltimore, August 16, 1945. ENOCH PRATT FREE LIBRARY/MARYLAND'S STATE LIBRARY RESOURCE CENTER

Newspapers being sold for five cents at Park Avenue and Lexington Street, May 7, 1945.
The headline read: "All Germany Surrenders." BALTIMORE SUN MEDIA GROUP

ABOVE: William Albert Feustle visiting Fort McHenry in Baltimore, 1948. He and his sweetheart, Edith Mae Gompf, would often dress up to go on dates and outings together. The pair later married on July 10, 1948. DEBORAH FEUSTLE BLAIR

RIGHT: Baltimore Polytechnic Institute student Edwin Wenderoth with his girlfriend, Louise Jenkins, June 9, 1946. COLLECTION 117, UNIVERSITY OF MARYLAND, BALTIMORE COUNTY

Joseph H. Cromwell, a telephone company rep, and James Pizzillo, a construction worker, putting the American flag on the 14th floor of the Chesapeake and Potomac Telephone building at 230 St. Paul Street, May 21, 1948. BALTIMORE SUN MEDIA GROUP

LEFT: Suburban Club members of the Jewish Welfare Board Armed Services Committee, September 17, 1950. Included are Ervin Brickhouse, Mrs. James Weinberg, Mrs. Harry Klotzman, and Ernest Charnock.
BALTIMORE SUN MEDIA GROUP

OPPOSITE: Baltimore schoolchildren touring the harbor, June 22, 1949. COLLECTION 117, UNIVERSITY OF MARYLAND, BALTIMORE COUNTY

RIGHT: General Sam Smith Park during Inner Harbor redevelopement, March 30, 1950. COLLECTION 117, UNIVERSITY OF MARYLAND, BALTIMORE COUNTY

OPPOSITE: Ellen Marie Dugan, Thomas Dugan, Henry C. Coe, Ward B. Coe, Theo, Johnny Lambert, and Mackee Lundberg with a horse at Baltimore County Humane Society, August 15, 1951.
COLLECTION 117, UNIVERSITY OF MARYLAND, BALTIMORE COUNTY

BELOW RIGHT: Members of Baltimore Bird Club on an outing, May 3, 1951.
COLLECTION 117, UNIVERSITY OF MARYLAND, BALTIMORE COUNTY

ABOVE: Dedication of Ambrose J. Kennedy playground, November 25, 1951. City Councilman Ambrose J. Kennedy Jr. acknowledged on behalf of the Kennedy family. COLLECTION 117, UNIVERSITY OF MARYLAND, BALTIMORE COUNTY

RIGHT: Girl Scouts clothing drive for Goodwill Industries, November 26, 1952. Betsy Boyd, Marcie Brown, Nancy Childs, Margaret Everett, Patsy Hoenes, Jane Hosking, Barbara Stafford, Marion Stafford, Mary Thomas, and Patricia McCormack are included. BALTIMORE SUN MEDIA GROUP

LEFT: The Baltimore Zoo's new elephant receiving a once-over from the Park Board, November 1953. ENOCH PRATT FREE LIBRARY/MARYLAND'S STATE LIBRARY RESOURCE CENTER

BELOW LEFT: Model Youth at City Council, May 6, 1954. COLLECTION 117, UNIVERSITY OF MARYLAND, BALTIMORE COUNTY

BELOW: Brownie Scouts painting Santa mugs at Hamilton Recreation Center, December 1952. Included are Norma Bond, Kathleen Powers, Elaine Stewart, Lynn Beichner, Mrs. James Florin, Lyn Schomp, Sandra Burgess, Martha Brichett, and Carolyn Sturdibant. COLLECTION 117, UNIVERSITY OF MARYLAND, BALTIMORE COUNTY

RIGHT: The 50th-anniversary celebration of Joseph T. McNaney and Marie McNaney at their home on Manor Road, 1959. In attendance were 25 of their 26 grandchildren. DOLORES "DEE" (MCNANEY) WALSH

OPPOSITE: Members of Box SHC Association, an all-black fire buff group, at their Baltimore headquarters located at 1813 McCulloh Street, September 1958. From left: James N. Smith, Mrs. Smith, Howard E. Gibson, Walter Turner, Delmar E. Darris, Zachary Kelly (mascot), Miss Linda Scott, Arthur P. Hardy, Charles Walker. The group had 18 members. COLLECTION 117, UNIVERSITY OF MARYLAND, BALTIMORE COUNTY

BELOW RIGHT: East Baltimore Boys Club holding crabs during a reunion, July 24, 1958. From left: Al C., Arnest Fink, Paul Wolman, Leonard A. A. Sems, Maryn D. Alexander. COLLECTION 117, UNIVERSITY OF MARYLAND, BALTIMORE COUNTY

BELOW: Children receiving a key during the community fund campaign, May 24, 1956. COLLECTION 117, UNIVERSITY OF MARYLAND, BALTIMORE COUNTY

FRANKLIN ELEM
SCHOOL
GRADE 6
MRS KRAJOVIC
JUNE 1956
BALTIMORE COUNTY
MARYLAND

CHAPTER EIGHT

Education

As it is now, Baltimore was a college town in the 1940s and 1950s. But it was a very different college town. Single-sex institutions were still widespread. The Johns Hopkins University would not admit women until 1970 and Loyola College would not admit them until 1971. Goucher College would not admit men until 1987.

Integration was progressing, but slowly. The University of Maryland, College Park enrolled its first African-American undergraduate, Hiram Whittle, in 1951. Whittle arrived in the midst of a rapid expansion for the state's flagship university, one that saw Byrd Stadium, Cole Field House, and McKeldin Library open between 1950 and 1958.

Johns Hopkins admitted its first black undergraduate, Frederick Scott, in 1945. Six years later, the university's renowned hospital became the launching point for another civil rights-era story when biologist George Otto Gey, acting without permission, cultivated a line of cancer cells from African-American patient Henrietta Lacks. These "HeLa" cells would prove essential to scientific research into the 21st century.

Meanwhile, Towson University was known as the Maryland State Teachers College at Towson, and training teachers was, in fact, its chief purpose until it expanded in the 1960s. Coppin State served a similar role and moved to its current location along North Avenue in 1952, two years after it officially became part of the state's higher education system.

Morgan State was not only a proud center of black culture in the city but an athletic powerhouse that sent a string of athletes, led by future Pro Football Hall of Famer Roosevelt "Rosey" Brown, to the professional ranks.

UMBC did not exist at all.

On the secondary front, the 1950s also brought desegregation to Baltimore's public schools in the wake of the U.S. Supreme Court's decision in *Brown v. Board of Education*. Baltimore Polytechnic Institute was an early battleground, with African-American students suing to gain entry to the school's prestigious college preparatory program in 1952. Backed by the NAACP, they won admission in a 5-3 vote by the city school board.

Neither Baltimore Polytechnic nor Baltimore City College admitted female students until the 1970s. Western High School served as a sister school to both.

City and Poly were already five decades into their famed football rivalry as the 1940s dawned, but the game moved to Thanksgiving Day in 1944 to avoid a conflict with the Army-Navy game and would remain a holiday tradition for several generations.

Just as desegregation would prove to be the dominant educational story of the 1950s, war lay at the heart of the previous decade's narrative.

The early 1940s saw a generation of young men depart for combat in World War II and a generation of young women mobilize to assist the war effort. These movements shaped the missions of area schools and universities in myriad ways.

As the war effort accelerated in 1942, the Johns Hopkins Applied Physics Laboratory was created out of a used-car garage in Silver Spring. With its evolution into a leading weapons developer, the APL would not only add to the university's research muscle, it would make Hopkins one of the richest educational institutions in the world.

After the war, the G.I. Bill sent millions of veterans into universities and other training programs, an educational flood that helped fuel the nation's rise to superpower status.

—*Childs Walker*

OPPOSITE: Sixth-grade class at Franklin Elementary School in Reisterstown, June 1956. The class was taught by Mrs. Krajovic.
COLLECTION OF BALTIMORE COUNTY PUBLIC LIBRARY, REISTERSTOWN BRANCH

RIGHT: University of Maryland cooks, late 1800s. BALTIMORE SUN MEDIA GROUP

OPPOSITE: Group of boys with MUS on shirts on parallel bars, circa 1920.
COLLECTION 137, P75-54-N133G, UNIVERSITY OF MARYLAND, BALTIMORE COUNTY

BELOW RIGHT: University of Maryland hockey team, 1897. BALTIMORE SUN MEDIA GROUP

BELOW: Franklin High School, 1901. Franklin Academy became Reisterstown High School in 1875 and Franklin High School in 1896.
BALTIMORE COUNTY PUBLIC LIBRARY, REISTERSTOWN BRANCH

ABOVE: Lacrosse practice at the Johns Hopkins University, March 7, 1931.
BALTIMORE SUN MEDIA GROUP

OPPOSITE: Stenography and typing class at James Lawrence Kernan Hospital and Industrial School of Maryland for Crippled Children, 1937. The hospital was founded in the mid-1800s by James Lawrence Kernan.
BALTIMORE SUN MEDIA GROUP

FAR RIGHT: Garden party at Goucher College, June 4, 1925. From left: Virginia Forwood, Audrey Noonan, Mary Graham, Virginia Fox.
BALTIMORE SUN MEDIA GROUP

RIGHT: Athletes from Mount Saint Joseph, 1921. COLLECTION 137, P75-54-N96G, UNIVERSITY OF MARYLAND, BALTIMORE COUNTY

ABOVE: Student decorating her freshman room at Goucher College, October 11, 1942. BALTIMORE SUN MEDIA GROUP

ABOVE LEFT: Youth studying at John Frederick Wiessner Orphan Asylum, 4915 Holder Avenue, Highlandtown, 1937. BALTIMORE SUN MEDIA GROUP

OPPOSITE: Student Edward Vargo and instructor George Bayer at Saint Mary's Industrial School Garage, December 14, 1941. BALTIMORE SUN MEDIA GROUP

LEFT: Goucher students waiting for the streetcar, October 2, 1942. BALTIMORE SUN MEDIA GROUP

ABOVE: Margaret Chambers, Mary Abell, Betty Sneeringer, Mary Pfaff, and Eleanor Green playing field hockey at Goucher College, November 21, 1943. BALTIMORE SUN MEDIA GROUP

OPPOSITE: City College rowing team, 1947. Included are Raymond Ely, George Mayo, Lee Hoffman, Robert Smelkin, Jack Nau, Jack Scherch, Lloyd Mailman, Jerry Reamer, and Jack Magner. COLLECTION 117, UNIVERSITY OF MARYLAND, BALTIMORE COUNTY

ABOVE: Catonsville Elementary School students, 1940s. BALTIMORE COUNTY PUBLIC LIBRARY, CATONSVILLE BRANCH

TOP: Goucher College students riding bicycles, November 18, 1946. BALTIMORE SUN MEDIA GROUP

OPPOSITE: City College vs. Polytechnic Institute football game, 1950. BALTIMORE SUN MEDIA GROUP

ABOVE: Jewish Educational Alliance nursery school graduation at 1216 East Baltimore Street, May 16, 1951. Shirley Weitzman, Phylis Perlman, Susan Walters, Marylou Roman, Sherlyn _, Jay Edwards Cohen, Paul Mazeroff, Alan Jay Blum, and Herbert Seigel are included. BALTIMORE SUN MEDIA GROUP

ABOVE RIGHT: Guilford School students, May 22, 1951. Included are Eileen Yosy, Betty Dale, Donna Lee Cole, Jay Franklin Spray Jr., Bimi Atwater, Timmy Cravens, Susan Bier, Allan Simmons, and George Jakovies. COLLECTION 117, UNIVERSITY OF MARYLAND, BALTIMORE COUNTY

RIGHT: Doughnuts and coffee being served to veterans in the VA building lobby of Baltimore Construction Institute, February 16, 1951. COLLECTION 117, UNIVERSITY OF MARYLAND, BALTIMORE COUNTY

Essex Elementary School, November 12, 1952. Mrs. Mary Maxwell, teacher, with parents and first-grade students in a drawing class.

RIGHT: Senior students Charles (age 17) and Norman (age 18) in front of a switchboard at Mergenthaler Vocational-Technical High School, April 20, 1953. COLLECTION 117, UNIVERSITY OF MARYLAND, BALTIMORE COUNTY

BELOW RIGHT: Bear Creek Elementary School students lining up to take the bus, September 27, 1955. COLLECTION 117, UNIVERSITY OF MARYLAND, BALTIMORE COUNTY

BELOW: Mrs. Mabel Mathews with her niece Gale Tyler (age five) and Robert Calkes (age six) with his mother Mrs. Janet Ostasewski with Dr. Mary S. Braun, the principal of Columbus School No. 99, on school registration day, August 31, 1954. BALTIMORE SUN MEDIA GROUP

LEFT: Booker T. Washington Junior High School student Gloria Lockerman helping revive the lost art of spelling, May 2, 1955. BALTIMORE SUN MEDIA GROUP

BELOW: Members of Western High School's graduating class before their final ceremonies, 1955. BALTIMORE SUN MEDIA GROUP

CHAPTER NINE

Civil Rights and Activism

I n May 1954, civil rights attorney Thurgood Marshall, a Baltimore native and descendant of slaves, won his most famous legal battle for equality. The U.S. Supreme Court ruled in a landmark case, *Brown v. Board of Education*, that "separate educational facilities are inherently unequal." Baltimore's school board quickly voted to desegregate the city schools and adopt a free choice policy that made integration voluntary.

Four months later, Walter Gill, a 17-year-old rising senior, became one of the first black students to enter the elite, all-white, all-male Baltimore City College High School. He and nine other black students took streetcars to the famous "Castle on the Hill" and found many of their white classmates accepting, if not warm, and unwilling to take part in the protests against integration that took place that fall around the city.

Walter Gill became the first black graduate of City College and went on to a long career as an educator. He was one of hundreds of pioneers across Baltimore who broke through racial barriers that had been in place for decades. Black students and civil rights activists, joined by some white supporters, demanded that restaurants and stores end their discriminatory practices. In January 1955, students from Morgan State University staged a sit-in of the Read's Drugstore at Lexington and Howard streets. The event lasted only about an hour but received national attention and, while the drug store is gone from the building that housed it, it is considered a hallowed place in Baltimore history.

The civil rights movement in the late 1940s and 1950s led to changes — the racial integration of civil service and labor unions, the desegregation of recreational facilities, public transportation, and accommodations, new laws that banned discrimination in housing, and the emergence of black political power and a black middle class. The movement came on the heels of a period of spirited activism for workers rights after World War II. Unionism in the mills in the city and Baltimore County was robust, and veterans demanded that they receive full benefits, including instruction in skilled trades.

Baltimoreans raised picket signs to protest the nuclear arms race during the Cold War. They marched against racial discrimination in downtown movie theaters and, in July 1963, they famously mounted a major demonstration against the whites-only admissions policy at the Gwynn Oak Amusement Park in Baltimore County.

In the 1950s, years of activism and hard-won racial progress, Baltimore's population was close to its historic peak of 950,000. But seismic changes were just starting to be felt — the loss of industry, the accelerated development of the suburbs, and a prolonged period of white flight that led to a steady decline in the city's population over the next six decades.

—*Dan Rodricks*

OPPOSITE: Police attempting to contain the chaos of crowds of protesters against school segregation, arresting both white and African-American protesters on Light Street, October 4, 1954. BALTIMORE SUN MEDIA GROUP

RIGHT: Women's suffrage activists in Baltimore, 1913.
BALTIMORE SUN MEDIA GROUP

BELOW RIGHT: Women's suffrage parade in Baltimore, 1913.
BALTIMORE SUN MEDIA GROUP

BELOW: Communists marching in Baltimore, March 7, 1930.
BALTIMORE SUN MEDIA GROUP

ABOVE: Baltimore Transit Company strike, December 16, 1942.
BALTIMORE SUN MEDIA GROUP

LEFT: Communists march on East Baltimore Street, January 24, 1931. Edward Bender, the district organizer, is in front in a leather coat. BALTIMORE SUN MEDIA GROUP

RIGHT: Veterans leaving War Memorial to march on Baltimore Construction Institute's Veterans Affairs office, February 15, 1951.
COLLECTION 117, UNIVERSITY OF MARYLAND, BALTIMORE COUNTY

BELOW RIGHT: Members of the VA council waiting for word on phone as to Baltimore Construction Institute's opening again in VA office lobby, February 16, 1951. COLLECTION 117, UNIVERSITY OF MARYLAND, BALTIMORE COUNTY

BELOW: Veterans protesting the closure of Baltimore Construction Institute in the lobby of the school's VA building, February 16, 1951.
COLLECTION 117, UNIVERSITY OF MARYLAND, BALTIMORE COUNTY

For the first time in Baltimore, public schools opened with white and blacks in same classes in 1954. Second-grader Charles Thompson was the only black child in a class of 40 pupils.
BALTIMORE SUN MEDIA GROUP

ABOVE RIGHT: James Donati, a striker at Bethlehem Steel, July 28, 1956. BALTIMORE SUN MEDIA GROUP

ABOVE LEFT: Integrated students of Public School No. 60 reciting the pledge of allegiance to the flag, June 26, 1955. BALTIMORE SUN MEDIA GROUP

OPPOSITE: Kindergarten teacher Miss Gwendolyn Michaels with her new integrated class at Baltimore School No. 99 on North and Washington Streets, September 7, 1954. BALTIMORE SUN MEDIA GROUP

LEFT: School kids in front of City Hall protesting integration, October 6, 1954. BALTIMORE SUN MEDIA GROUP

RIGHT: James Hunter (age 11) and Louis Harris (age 16) jumping off the high board together at Druid Hill Park Pool No. 1 as the city opened the pool on an integrated basis for the first time, June 23, 1956. BALTIMORE SUN MEDIA GROUP

BELOW: Carol Anderson being escorted into school by her father, September 5, 1957. BALTIMORE SUN MEDIA GROUP

Protesters of atom bomb testing marching on Franklin Street in Baltimore, May 29, 1958. BALTIMORE SUN MEDIA GROUP

CHAPTER TEN

Recreation and Celebration

Has any time in the city's lore shaped Baltimore sports more than the aftermath of World War II? Two big league teams — the Colts and Orioles — emerged in the 1940s and 1950s to tout the city's growing swagger. Never mind that they faltered at first; hungry fans embraced their big-time ties.

The Colts arrived in 1947 and played three years in the short-lived All-America Football Conference before joining the National Football League for one dismal (1-11) season and disbanding. Revived in 1953, they peaked five years later, winning the 1958 championship, 23-17, over the Giants in New York in sudden-death overtime — perhaps the seminal game in NFL history. The Colts repeated the following year, rallying in the fourth quarter to defeat the Giants, 31-16, before a jubilant home crowd of 57,545 who stormed the field, tore down goal posts and salvaged planks from the Colts bench as souvenirs. Fans revered the likes of Johnny Unitas, Raymond Berry, Lenny Moore, and Art Donovan. Sellouts were a given; Colts fans, fervid.

In 1954, the Orioles returned to the American League after a 51-year absence. To welcome them, on Opening Day, the city put on the Ritz, staging a 90-minute parade with 22 brass bands and 33 floats that tooted their way down 3.5 miles of orchid-strewn streets, past a cheering throng of 350,000 people. At spanking new Memorial Stadium, decked out with 2.5 miles of red, white, and blue bunting, the Orioles won their home opener, then plummeted to finish the season 54-100. But they drew 1,060,910 fans, more than three times the 1953 attendance of their predecessors, the St. Louis Browns. Twelve years later, the team captured its first world championship.

The minor league Orioles had set the stage in 1944, winning the Junior World Series and the hearts of their faithful after the loss of Oriole Park, which burned to the ground July 4. The team played out the year at Municipal Stadium, on Thirty-Third Street, where one game of the championship series against the Louisville Colonels drew an October crowd of 52,833, a then-record attendance for a minor league contest. Two months later, on a crisp, cold Saturday afternoon, 70,000 football fans squeezed into the stadium to watch Army, led by Doc Blanchard and Glenn Davis, defeat Navy, 23-7, for the national championship.

Meanwhile, two miles away on Hillen Road, Morgan State continued its dynastic grip on black college football. Coach Eddie Hurt's team won every Colored Intercollegiate Athletic Association title from 1940 to 1944 and outscored opponents 120-0 in 1943.

Baltimore made headlines in other sports, too. Four years after they began play at the Coliseum, the Bullets won the Basketball Association of America championship in 1948. Swept into the NBA the following season, the Bullets sputtered along until 1954 when they disbanded, to return in 1963.

—*Mike Klingaman*

OPPOSITE: Clifton Park swimming pool, June 24, 1952. BALTIMORE SUN MEDIA GROUP

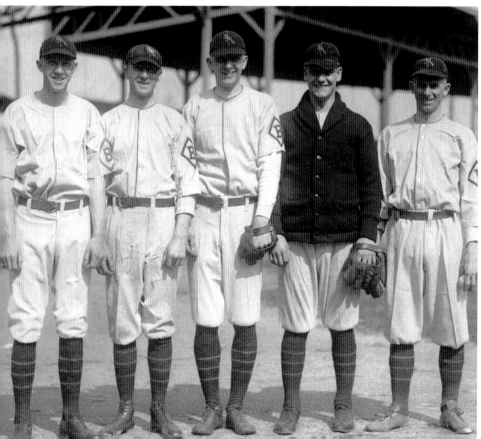

LEFT: Crowd watching a baseball game at Clifton Park, May 9, 1932.
COLLECTION 117, UNIVERSITY OF MARYLAND, BALTIMORE COUNTY

OPPOSITE TOP: Laying the cornerstone of the Masonic Temple, November 20, 1866.
BALTIMORE SUN MEDIA GROUP

OPPOSITE BOTTOM LEFT: Baltimore Orioles baseball team, April 21, 1923.
BALTIMORE SUN MEDIA GROUP

OPPOSITE BOTTOM RIGHT: Celebrating Baltimore's Sesquicentennial, October 11–19, 1880. BALTIMORE SUN MEDIA GROUP

BELOW LEFT: Ticket buyers lining up at a downtown movie house which drew a capacity audience, December 15, 1930. Mr. Rome arranged the performances for the benefit of the unemployed in Baltimore.
COLLECTION 117, UNIVERSITY OF MARYLAND, BALTIMORE COUNTY

BELOW: Mary Bradburn, Anna Bradburn, Betty Fioresta, Hilda Burch, and Myrtle Bardburn watching the Chesapeake Bay Workboat Races, June 24, 1930.
BALTIMORE SUN MEDIA GROUP

ABOVE: Armistice Day Parade at Hopkins Place and Baltimore Street, 1934. ENOCH PRATT FREE LIBRARY/MARYLAND'S STATE LIBRARY RESOURCE CENTER

OPPOSITE: Children playing at the Clifton Park playground, March 7, 1933. COLLECTION 117, UNIVERSITY OF MARYLAND, BALTIMORE COUNTY

Babe Ruth watching a polo match, April 19, 1936. BALTIMORE SUN MEDIA GROUP

ABOVE: An exhilarating ride on the Mountain Speedway at Carlins Park on Memorial Day, 1939. BALTIMORE SUN MEDIA GROUP

ABOVE LEFT: Fishermen in the second annual Chesapeake Bay Fishing Fair, 1937. Baltimorean William Wholey, of 1236 Riverside Avenue, was awarded the champion fish caller. BALTIMORE SUN MEDIA GROUP

LEFT: War Admiral defeating rival Pompoon at the Preakness, May 17, 1937. BALTIMORE SUN MEDIA GROUP

LEFT: Dancing at Cahill Recreation Center, March 20, 1945. COLLECTION 117, UNIVERSITY OF MARYLAND, BALTIMORE COUNTY

OPPOSITE: Launching of the USS *Patrick Henry* from Bethlehem Steel's shipyard in Baltimore on Liberty Fleet Day, September 27, 1941. It was the first Liberty ship to launch. President Franklin D. Roosevelt was in attendance and gave a speech during the launch. ENOCH PRATT FREE LIBRARY/MARYLAND'S STATE LIBRARY RESOURCE CENTER

BELOW LEFT AND BELOW: Army–Navy football game at Baltimore Municipal Stadium in front of a sold-out crowd of 66,659, December 2, 1944. Army was victorious in the "game of the century," winning 23-7. BALTIMORE SUN MEDIA GROUP

Clifton Park swimming pool, June 20, 1948. COLLECTION 117, UNIVERSITY OF MARYLAND, BALTIMORE COUNTY

ABOVE: Joe Walker, John Walker, Pat, and George Roth playing chess at Patterson Park on Biddle Street, July 19, 1949. COLLECTION 117, UNIVERSITY OF MARYLAND, BALTIMORE COUNTY

LEFT: Children playing in a fountain at Canton Playground's wading pool, July 27, 1949. COLLECTION 117, UNIVERSITY OF MARYLAND, BALTIMORE COUNTY

ABOVE: Catonsville Boy Scouts, circa 1950. COLLECTION OF BALTIMORE COUNTY PUBLIC LIBRARY, CATONSVILLE BRANCH

OPPOSITE: Crowds awaiting fireworks for July Fourth celebrations, 1952. BALTIMORE SUN MEDIA GROUP

ABOVE: Pat Yeager helping Richard Szyjka do a shoulder stand at Latrobe Park, July 10, 1952.
COLLECTION 117, UNIVERSITY OF MARYLAND, BALTIMORE COUNTY

ABOVE RIGHT: Children skating and sledding on ice that came from a water leak at 1530 Madeira Street, March 3, 1950. COLLECTION 117, UNIVERSITY OF MARYLAND, BALTIMORE COUNTY

OPPOSITE: Little League baseball game in Catonsville, 1950s.
COLLECTION OF BALTIMORE COUNTY PUBLIC LIBRARY, CATONSVILLE BRANCH

RIGHT: Playing on the 400 block of Fawcett Street, June 17, 1952. COLLECTION 117, UNIVERSITY OF MARYLAND, BALTIMORE COUNTY

RIGHT: Leone's Cafe baseball team, August 24, 1954.
COLLECTION 117, UNIVERSITY OF MARYLAND, BALTIMORE COUNTY

BELOW RIGHT: Thousands of people lining Baltimore Street to cheer their city's new entry in the American League, April 16, 1954. Major league baseball was back in Baltimore after an absence of 52 years after the St. Louis Browns were sold to a syndicate led by team president Clarence Miles for $2.5 million in December 1953. BALTIMORE SUN MEDIA GROUP

ABOVE: Roger Griswold at Memorial Stadium, 1957. BALTIMORE SUN MEDIA GROUP

ABOVE LEFT: I Am An American Day Parade, September 17, 1956. BALTIMORE SUN MEDIA GROUP

LEFT: Dedication of Memorial Stadium, June 1, 1956. From left: James Anderson, Ted Williams, Mayor Thomas D'Alesandro Jr., unidentified . BALTIMORE SUN MEDIA GROUP

ABOVE: Gil McDougald, Billy O'Dell, and Nelson "Nellie" Fox at the Major League Baseball All-Star Game in Baltimore, July 8, 1958.
BALTIMORE SUN MEDIA GROUP

RIGHT: Vice President Richard Nixon throwing out the first pitch to Gus Triandos at the All-Star Game held at Memorial Stadium, July 8, 1958.
BALTIMORE SUN MEDIA GROUP

LEFT: Bainbridge Girls marching in the I Am An American Day Parade, September 15, 1958. BALTIMORE SUN MEDIA GROUP

BELOW LEFT: The Florida winter league for the Orioles, December 20, 1959. Front row, from left: Chuck Hinton, John "Boog" Powell, Dave Nicholson. Back row: Art Quirk, Leo Burke, Bob Saverine, Steve Barber. BALTIMORE SUN MEDIA GROUP

BELOW: Governor Theodore Roosevelt McKeldin, Edward J. Morris, and Archbishop Francis P. Keogh attending a St. Patrick's Day Parade, March 18, 1958. BALTIMORE SUN MEDIA GROUP

ABOVE: Baltimore Colts vs. New York Giants Championship Game at Memorial Stadium on December 27, 1959. Colts' Linebacker Bill Pellington barrels into Giants' Frank Gifford and halts him in the fourth quarter. BALTIMORE SUN MEDIA GROUP

ABOVE LEFT: Colts' Championship Game against the New York Giants at Memorial Stadium, December 27, 1959. Johnny Unitas watches the measurement on the Colts' 4-yard line: 1st down. BALTIMORE SUN MEDIA GROUP

OPPOSITE: Elephants parading at Baltimore and Liberty Streets during the Cristiani Bros Circus, May 12, 1959. BALTIMORE SUN MEDIA GROUP

LEFT: Colts vs. New York Giants Championship Game December 27, 1959. Colts' quarterback Johnny Unitas keeps the ball and races four yards to paydirt early in the fourth quarter. The touchdown put the Colts ahead of the Giants, 13-9. Helping out on the play is Lenny Moore with a neat block on Giant linebacker Cliff Livingston (89). BALTIMORE SUN MEDIA GROUP

Index